Soldiers of the Union!

You defended and saved our Country in time of her greatest trial.

To-day, you need a protection for your families and homes. You can secure it by taking a policy of life insurance in the

Massachusetts Mutual Life Ins. Company
OF SPRINGFIELD, MASS.

Do not insure until you examine it.

All policies are NON-FORFEITABLE after two years. PAID UP AND CASH VALUES on every contract. Best policy for the insured.

Assets, . . $10,415,817.64
Liabilities, . 9,558,475.63
Surplus, . . . 857,342.01

Writes more new business every year than any other Massachusetts Company. Partnership insurance a specialty.

For information and circulars, address Home Office,
Springfield, Mass.

M. V. B. Edgerly, President.   John A. Hall, Secretary

CALENDAR

OF THE

CIVIL WAR

INCLUDING ...

EVERY MILITARY AND NAVAL ENGAGEMENT (EXCEPT THE SMALLEST SKIRMISHES), THE SECESSION CONVENTIONS, PRESIDENTIAL NOMINATIONS, CALLS FOR TROOPS, PEACE NEGOTIATIONS, IMPORTANT ARMY MOVEMENTS, AND OTHER EVENTS OF INTEREST

PRICE, 10 CENTS

BOSTON
PRESS OF ROCKWELL & CHURCHILL
1890

Attributed to
Raymond L. Bridgman

Media Hatchery
Orchard Park, NY

All text and illustrations in this publication are in the public domain and were obtained from the Library of Congress. All other text, design, and formatting are
© 2021 by William C. Even — Media Hatchery.

All rights reserved.

ISBN: 978-1-955180-00-9 (Paperback Edition)

Front cover:
Yorktown, Va., May 1862. A scene during the Civil War
Photographer — Mathew B. Brady
Obtained from the Library of Congress
Prints and Photographs Division.

Printed and bound in the United States of America
First Printing 2021

Published by Media Hatchery
P. O. Box 554
Orchard Park, NY 14127

MediaHatchery.com

DEDICATION.

To my father, William — an extraordinary husband, father, and grandfather; a magnificent, gifted artist; a wonderful human being; and a Civil War enthusiast.

Pa, I miss you every day.

— William C. Even, Media Hatchery

JANUARY.

1. — Mason and Slidell sailed for England, '62. Emancipation proclamation took effect; Galveston captured by Magruder, '63. Sloop of war San Jacinto lost off Florida, '65.

2. — Gov. Ellis of North Carolina seized government property, '61. Battle of Stone River or Murfreesboro' ended, '63.

3. — Florida state convention, '61. Slight action at Moorefield, Va., '63. Action at Jonesville, Va., '64.

4. — National fast day by presidential proclamation, not observed in the South, '61. Bragg abandoned Murfreesboro', '63.

5. — Confederate fort captured on Little River, N.C., '63. End at Vicksburg of Grierson's raid, '64.

6. — Kirby Smith put in command of confederate troops west of the Mississippi River, '64.

7. — Alabama and Mississippi conventions, '61. Battle of Blue Gap, Va., '62. 1,600 Indians attacked Julesburg, Col., '65.

8. — Secretary Thompson, of the Interior department, resigned, '61. Action at Springfield, Mo., '63. Loyal mass meeting in New Orleans to form free state government, '64. Gen. B. F. Butler removed from command of the army of the James, '65.

9. — Mississippi seceded, 84 to 15; Star of the West fired upon at Charleston, '61. 20,000 men exchanged, '63.

Confederate government conscripted every man in Cleveland, Tenn., '64.

10. — Florida seceded, 62 to 7, '61. Battle of Middle Creek, Ky.; Senators Johnson and Polk expelled from the United States senate, '62. Cavalry fight at Strawberry Plain, '64.

11. — Alabama seceded, 61 to 39; Secretary Thomas, of the Treasury, resigned; the governor of Louisiana seized government property; New York pledged its whole support to the national government, '61. Battle at Fort Hindman, Ark., '63. Longstreet, with 46,000 men, fortified at Bull's Gap, Tenn.; meeting in New York to aid people in Savannah; F. P. Blair, sr., arrived in Richmond on a peace mission, '64.

12. — Confederate raid on Holly Springs, Miss., '63. Gen. Marston raided successfully in Virginia, '64.

13. — Pensacola navy yard surrendered by Com. Armstrong, '61. Simon Cameron resigned as secretary of war, and Edwin M. Stanton was appointed, '62. Second attack on Fort Fisher, '65.

14. — Gunboat Queen of the West captured in the Red River by the confederates; battle of Bayou Teche, La., '63.

15. — Mound City, Ark., burned to clear out guerrillas, '63. Fort Fisher captured, '65.

16. — The Crittenden compromise defeated by Clark's substitute that the constitution was good enough, and that secession ought to be put down, '61. Pirate Oreto escaped from Mobile, '63. Magazine exploded at Fort Fisher, '64. F. P. Blair, sr., returned to Washington; Forts Caswell

and Campbell, N.C., evacuated and blown up by the confederates, '65.

17. — Pollockville, N.C., taken, '63. Action near Bainbridge, Tenn., '64. Monitor Patapsco sunk off Charleston by confederate torpedo, '65.

18. — The Massachusetts legislature pledged its whole support to the government; Virginia appropriated $1,000,000 for defence, '61. Two blockade runners captured by Admiral Porter, '65.

19. — Georgia seceded, 208 to 89, A. H. Stephens and Herschel V. Johnson voting no, '61. Battle of Mills Springs, Ky., Zollicoffer, confederate commander, killed, '62.

20. — Gen. Woodbury's expedition (Union) to Ponta Rosa, '64. F. P. Blair, sr., went to Richmond the second time, '65.

21. — Alabama congressmen resigned; Jefferson Davis left the senate, '61. Fitz John Porter dismissed from the service, '63.

22. — Burnside failed to cross the Rappahannock, '63.

23. — Georgia congressmen resigned, '61. Stone fleet sunk in Charleston harbor, '62. Successful Union raids in Virginia and North Carolina, '64.

24. — Augusta arsenal seized by the state, '61. Battle of Woodbury, Tenn., '63. Gen. Rhoddy, confederate, driven across the Tennessee with loss of trains and supplies, '64. Holiday in Louisiana to celebrate the abolition of slavery in Louisiana, Maryland, Tennessee, and Missouri, '65.

25. — Organization of the first colored volunteers at Port Royal, '63. Maj. Burroughs, guerrilla, shot while es-

caping from Fortress Monroe, '64. Savannah meeting to thank New York; Gen. Lee issued a call to arms, '65.

26. — Louisiana seceded, 113 to 17, '61. Hooker succeeded Burnside in command of the Potomac army, '63. Debate in the confederate house on enlisting negroes, '65.

27. — Bombardment of Fort McAllister, Ga., '63. Union cavalry victory at Sevierville, '64. Blair returned from second peace mission; confederates fired Savannah, Ga., '65.

28. — Texas convention, '61. Large meeting at Nashville, Tenn., to restore state government, '64. Confederate house passed bill for employment of negroes, '65.

29. — Gen. Banks promulgated emancipation proclamation at New Orleans, '63. Confederate attack on Cumberland Gap defeated, '64.

30. — Floyd indicted for malfeasance and conspiracy, '61. Union supply train captured near Petersburg, Va., '64. A. H. Stephens, Gen. R. M. T. Hunter, and Judge Campbell came within Grant's lines as peace commissioners, '65.

31. — Three ironclads attacked Charleston blockaders, one sunk; attack on United States troops in Indiana arresting deserters, '63. Lee made general-in-chief of the confederate armies; thirteenth amendment adopted, '65.

FEBRUARY.

1. — New Orleans mint and custom-house seized; secession of Texas submitted to popular vote, 166 to 7, '61. Second attack on Fort McAllister, Ga., '63. Battle of Cumberland Iron Works, Tenn.; Lincoln ordered draft of 500,000 men on March 10, '64. Secretary Seward left Washington to meet confederate peace commissioners at Fortress Monroe, '65.

2. — Queen of the West ran the Vicksburg blockade, '63. Gen. Scammon and staff captured by confederates on the steamship Levi, '64. Lincoln met confederate peace commissioners at Fortress Monroe; gold at 4400 premium at Richmond, '65.

3. — The steamer Nashville ordered out of Southampton (Eng.) harbor; Senator Bright of Indiana expelled from the United States senate, '62. Confederate attack on Donelson defeated, '63. Sherman, with 25,000 men, crossed the Big Black and reached Bolton, '64.

4. — Delegates at Montgomery, Ala., to form a confederate government, '61. Governor-general of Canada signed the bill to prevent confederate raids across the border, '65.

5. — Skirmish on Bear Creek, Mo., '63. Expedition left Port Royal, '64. Battle of Hatcher's Run, Va., '65.

6. — Fort Henry captured by Grant and Foote, '62. Col. Cushman (confederate cotton-burner) captured near Ripley, Tenn., '63. Army of the Potomac reconnoitered in force toward Orange Court-House; Sherman moved south from Vicksburg, '64. Battle of fifth corps and Gregg's cavalry with confederates (Union victory), '65.

7. — Montgomery convention adopted provisional constitution, '61. Battle of Roanoke Island, '62.

8. — United States arsenal at Little Rock surrendered, '61. Confederate meeting at Dalton and Decatur, '64. Electoral votes counted in congress, — 212 for Lincoln and Johnson, and 21 for McClellan and Pendleton, '65.

9. — Jefferson Davis and A. H. Stephens elected provisional president and vice-president of the confederacy, '61. Gen. Rosecrans ordered the summary execution of confederates in Union uniform, '63. Action at Morgan's Mill, Ark., '64.

10. — Fight at Old River, La., '63. Col. Streight and 110 other Union officers escaped from Libby prison by tunnelling, '64. Sherman's right column, in part, landed on James Island, near Charleston, '65.

11. — Gens. Grierson and Smith began raid through Mississippi, '64. Gen. Terry reconnoitered in force toward Wilmington, '65.

12. — The gunboat Indianola ran the Vicksburg batteries, '63.

13. — Lincoln and Hamlin officially declared elected, '61.

14. — Union cavalry surprised at Anandale, Va.; Queen of the West lost, '63. Sherman occupied Meridian, Miss., and destroyed the state arsenal and much property, '64.

15. — Cavalry engagement near Gainesville, Tenn., '63.

16. — Fort Donelson taken with Gens. Buckner and Tilghman, '62.

17. — Confederates captured a forage train near Romney, Va., '63. Sherman occupied Columbia, S.C., and confederates evacuated Charleston, '65.

18. — Jefferson Davis inaugurated at Richmond, '61. Mortar boats opened fire on Vicksburg; copperhead state convention at Frankfort, Ky., dispersed, '63. Charleston occupied by Union troops, '65.

19. — Confederate congress met at Richmond; confederates seized Fort Keane, Kan., '61. Hopefield (opposite Memphis) burned by Gen. Hurlbut's order, '63. Fort Anderson, N.C., captured by Schofield and Porter, '65.

20. — Gunboat reconnaissance up the Rappahannock, '63. Battle of Olustee, Fla.; Gen. Seymour's expedition (Union) badly defeated at Sanderson, Fla., and Smith's expedition repulsed, '64. Gen. Cox defeated the confederates near Wilmington, N.C.; confederate house passed bill to arm negroes, '65.

21. — Jefferson Davis appointed his cabinet, '61. Battle of Valverde, N. Mex., '62. Confederates evacuated Wilmington, N.C., '65.

22. — Michael Hahn elected governor of Louisiana, '64. Union troops occupied Wilmington, N.C., '65.

23. — Confederates evacuated Nashville, '62. Forrest's attack on Smith repulsed, '64. Georgetown and Fort White, S.C., occupied by Union troops, '65.

24. — The Indianola captured near Grand Gulf, Miss., by four confederate steamers, '63. Burning of Columbia, S.C., '65.

25. — Cavalry fight near Hartwood church, Va., '63. (Feb. 25 to 27) battle of Buzzard's Roost, Ga., '64. Johnston took command as Beauregard's successor, '65.

26. — Cherokee national council repealed secession ordinance and abolished slavery, '63. Grierson and Smith returned to Memphis after a successful expedition, '64.

27. — The peace congress submitted a plan to the senate, '61. Sherman returned to Vicksburg after a 22 days' raid, '64.

28. — Confederate ironclad Nashville was captured in Ogeechee River, '63. Col. Richardson, guerrilla, was captured near the Cumberland River; Kilpatrick started on a raid in Virginia, '64.

29. — Kilpatrick's raid continued, Stevensburg to Richmond, extended to March 4, '64.

MARCH.

1. — Fight near Bradyville, Tenn.; Duke's guerrillas routed, '63. Confederate salt-works at St. Marks, Fla., destroyed, '64.

2. — Gen. F. W. Lander died; action at Pittsburg Landing, Tenn., '62. Sheridan captured nearly all of Early's force near Staunton, Va., '65.

3. — Sheridan defeated Van Dorn at Shelbyville, '63. Fort McAllister, Ga., again bombarded fruitlessly, '63. Grant made commander-in-chief over Halleck, '64. Skirmish between Sherman's and Wade Hampton's cavalry, '65.

4. — Lincoln inaugurated, '61. Battle of Memphis Station, Tenn.; battle of Thompson's Station, Tenn., '63. Col. Dahlgren murdered, '64. Lincoln inaugurated, '65.

5. — Beauregard took command of the army of the Mississippi; battle of Pea Ridge, Ark., from March 5 to 8, '62. Battle in Yazoo City, '64.

6. — Gen. Hunter ordered negroes drafted in the South, '63. Sherman's army crossed the Pearl River at Jackson, '64. Successful Union expedition up the Rappahannock, '65.

7. — Return of successful Union scouting expedition from Belle Plain, Va., '63. Sherman's cavalry occupied Brandon, '64.

8. — The Congress and the Cumberland sunk by the Confederate ram Merrimac, '62. Mosby captured Gen. Stoughton, '63. Confederate senate passed negro enlistment bill, '65.

9. — Engagement of Monitor and Merrimac, '62. Slight action below Port Hudson, '63. Sherman at Hillsboro'; Grant commissioned lieut.-gen., '64.

10. — Jacksonville, Fla., captured by the first South Carolina colored regiment, '63. Red River expedition embarked at Vicksburg, '64. Action at Wilcox's Bridge, N.C.; defeat of confederate Gen. Bragg at Kinston, N.C.; Grant forbade trade at points within confederate lines in Virginia, North Carolina, South Carolina, and Georgia, '65.

11. — McClellan removed, Halleck assigned to the department of the Mississippi, and Fremont to mountain department, '62. Hoke's confederate division defeated at Kinston, N.C., '65.

12. — Successful Union reconnaissance from Franklin, Tenn., '63. Grant appointed commander-in-chief of the armies of the United States, '64. Schofield occupied Kinston, '65.

13. — Battle of New Madrid, Mo., '62. Fort Greenwood on the Tallahatchie, Tenn., silenced by gun-boats, '63. Indianola evacuated by Union troops, '64. Sheridan destroyed the railroad between Richmond and Hanover, '65.

14. — Battle of Newbern, N.C., '62. Admiral Farragut, with seven vessels, passed Port Hudson after a fierce engagement, '63. Fort De Russy captured; call for 200,000 men for three years, '64.

15. — The Jeffersonian office at Richmond, Ind., destroyed by soldiers, '63. The confederate house, 36 to 32, suspended the habeas corpus act, '65.

MARCH.

16. — Union victory at Cumberland Mountain, '62. Union victory near Fort Pillow, '64. Arkansas voted herself a free state, '64. Union victory at Averysborough, N.C., '65.

17. — Fitzhugh Lee's cavalry defeated at Kelly's Ford, Va., '63. Fort De Russy blown up, '64. Gen. Canby moved against Mobile, '65.

18. — The Nashville escaped from Beaufort, S.C.; battle at Salem, Ark., '62. Confederate congress adjourned, '65.

19. — Steamer Georgiana, with arms for the confederates, destroyed off Charleston, '63. Confederate attack on Port Royal failed, '64. Union victory at Bentonville, N.C., '65.

20. — Battle of Vaught's Hill, near Milton, Tenn., '63.

21. — Fight at Cottage Grove, Tenn., '63. Confederate raid on Magnolia, '64. Junction of armies under Sherman, Terry, and Schofield; Wilson's cavalry defeated Roddy's cavalry at Marion and Plantersville; Goldsboro', N.C., taken by Union troops, '65.

22. — Mount Sterling, Ky., captured by guerrillas, '63. Ferguson's guerrillas massacred 24 Union cavalrymen at Johnson's Mills, Tenn., '64.

23. — Battle of Winchester, Va., '62. Action at Calf Killer Creek, Tenn., '64.

24. — Pontachoula, La., taken by Union troops, '63. Union City, Mo., attacked by Forrest, '64.

25. — Rams Lancaster and Switzerland lost in running Vicksburg batteries, '63. Owen Lovejoy died, aged 53, '64. Battle of Fort Steadman (before Petersburg), '65.

26. — Action at Apache Cañon, 26th to 28th, '62. Burnside took command of the department of the Ohio, '63. Forrest sacked Paducah, Ky.; Col. Clayton's victory at Longview, Ark., '64.

27. — Fast day in the confederacy, '63. Investment of Spanish Fort, the principal defence of Mobile, '65.

28. — Louisiana popular vote on secession, 20,448 yes, to 17,296 no, '61. Union victory at Cane River, '64. Attack on the defences of Mobile, '65.

29. — Blockade runners captured at Poplar Creek, Md., '63. Confederate ram Stonewall ordered to leave Lisbon; United States war steamer Niagara fired upon by Portuguese authorities; action at Quaker Rood, Va., '65.

30. — Mississippi convention ratified the confederate constitution, 78 to 7, '61. Battle near Somerset, Ky., Union victory, '63. Copperhead riot at Charleston and Mattoon, Ill., '64. Fighting before Richmond, '65.

31. — Gen. Heron appointed to the command of the army of the frontier, '63. Union victory at Crump's Hill, '64. Confederate victory before Richmond, '65.

APRIL.

1. — Farragut passed the Grand Gulf batteries with the Hartford, Switzerland, and Albatross, '63. Confederate ram Tennessee sunk near Grant's Pass, '64. Union victory at Five Forks, '65.

2. — Women's bread riot at Richmond, Va., '63. Action at Spoonville, Ark.; Forrest defeated Grierson near Summerville, '64. Grant advanced on Petersburg; heavy fighting; Richmond and Petersburg evacuated by night; Jefferson Davis left at 8 P.M.; capture of Selma, Ala., '65.

3. — South Carolina convention ratified the confederate constitution, 114 to 16, '61. Arrest of Knights of the Golden Circle in Reading, Pa., '63. Action at Okalona, Ark.; Petersburg occupied by Union troops at 4 A.M., and Richmond at 7 A.M., '65.

4. — Virginia convention refused, 89 to 45, to submit the secession ordinance to the people, '61. Slavery abolished in the District of Columbia, '62. New York metropolitan sanitary fair opened; Sheridan made cavalry commander of Potomac army, '64. Lincoln in Richmond, '65.

5. — Troops sent from Newbern to rescue Gen. Foster, '63. Action at Roseville, Ark.; confederate Gen. W. P. White assassinated by his own men, '64. Jefferson Davis proclaimed the evacuation of Richmond, and that they would never abandon one state of the confederacy, '65.

6. — Battle of Pittsburg Landing; Gen. A. S. Johnston killed, '62. Confederate Gen. Buford attacked Fort Halleck, Columbus, Ky., '64. Battle of Deatonsville between Grant and Lee, '65.

7. — Communication with Fort Sumter cut off, '61. Island No. 10 surrendered, '62. Dupont's bombardment of Sumter failed, '63. Action at Wilson's Farm, La.; fight with Lee at Farmville, '65.

8. — State department refused to recognize confederate commissioners, '61. Gen. Stoneman defeated at the battle of Pleasant Grove, La.; Gen. Franklin, of Banks's expedition, defeated at Mansfield, La., '64. Lee concentrated his army at Appomattox Court-House, Va.; battle of Appomattox (8th-9th), '65.

9. — Pascagoula, Miss., taken by Union troops and abandoned, '63. Lee surrendered; Spanish Fort, near Mobile, and other forts, captured, '65.

10. — Fort Pulaski surrendered, '62. Battle of Franklin, Tenn., '63. Action at Prairie D'Ann (10th-13th), Ark., '64. Evacuation of Mobile begun, '65.

11. — Surrender of Sumter demanded, '61. Union troops under Gen. Q. A. Gillmore captured Fort Pulaski, Ga., '62. Montgomery, Ala., surrendered to Gen. Wilson, '65.

12. — Beginning of the war — Sumter bombarded; Pennsylvania appropriated $500,000 to arm the state, '61. Action at Pleasant Hill Landing, La., '64. Capture of Fort Pillow and murder of the garrison, '64. Mobile occupied by Union troops; Stoneman defeated 3,000 confederates at Grant's Creek, '65.

13. — Sumter surrendered, '61. Battle of Irish Bend, La., 12th to 14th, '63. Action at Moscow, Ark., '64. Sherman occupied Raleigh, N.C., '65.

APRIL.

14. — Bombardment of Fort Pillow, '62. Battle of Bayou Teche, La., '63. Gunboat expedition from Butler's army captured prisoners and stores at Smithfield, Va., '64. President Lincoln shot by J. Wilkes Booth in Ford's theatre, Washington, '65.

15. — Lincoln's proclamation for 75,000 volunteers issued; extra session of congress called; New York legislature voted 30,000 men and $3,000,000, '61. Action at Liberty, Ark.; gunboat Chenango exploded, '64. President Lincoln died at 7.22 A.M.; Vice-President Johnson sworn in as president, '65.

16. — Confederate government called for 32,000 troops; Govs. Magoffin of Kentucky, and Letcher of Virginia, refuse to furnish troops to the federal government; action at Lee's Hills, Va., '61. Admiral Porter's fleet ran the Vicksburg batteries, '63. Columbus, Ga., captured, '65.

17. — Virginia seceded, 60 to 53, the result to be submitted to the people; Jefferson Davis issued letters of marque; the Massachusetts Sixth regiment started for Washington, '61. Col. Grierson's cavalry raid (ended May 3 at Baton Rouge, La.) began from Lagrange, Tenn., '63. Mosby surrendered to Hancock, '65.

18. — Pennsylvania volunteers in Washington; Harper's Ferry arsenal burned to save it from the confederates; two men killed by the confederates, '61. Bombardment of Forts Jackson and St. Philip below New Orleans, '62. Action at Poison Springs, Ark.; Baltimore sanitary fair opened, '64. Truce between Sherman and Johnston, '65.

19. — Attack on the Massachusetts Sixth regiment in Baltimore, four men killed and seven wounded; eleven of

the mob killed and many wounded; blockade of southern ports, '61. Battle of Camden, N.C., '62. Lincoln's funeral, '65.

20. — Confederates seized U.S. arsenal at Liberty, Mo., '61. Fight at Patterson, Mo., '63. Gen. Wessels surrendered Plymouth, N.C., to confederates, '64. Macon, Ga., occupied; Gen. Howell Cobb and others captured, '65.

21. — Norfolk navy yard destroyed; Union government took the Philadelphia and Baltimore railroad, '61. Saltworks near Wilmington, N.C., destroyed, '64. Gen. E. Kirby Smith proclaimed that he could continue the rebellion; Sherman's truce disapproved by the authorities, '65.

22. — Arsenals at Fayetteville, N.C., and Napoleon, Ark., seized by the confederates; Vermont legislature in extra session, '61.

23. — First South Carolina regiment started for the Potomac, '61. New York metropolitan sanitary fair closed; Grant received the sword by vote of 30,291 to 14,509 for McClellan, '64. Jefferson Davis fled to Georgia, '65.

24. — Fort Smith, Ark., seized by confederates; Virginia proclaimed a member of the confederacy, '61. Union fleet passed Forts Jackson and St. Philip, '62. Tuscumbia, Ala., occupied by Union troops, '63. Battle at Cane River, '64.

25. — New Orleans evacuated by the confederates; Fort Macon surrendered, '62. Confederate batteries at Duck River shoals in the Tennessee River silenced by gunboats, '63. Action at Marks' Mills, Ark., '64.

26. — Cape Girardeau, Mo., attacked unsuccessfully by confederates under Marmaduke, '62. Johnston surren-

dered 29,900 men to Sherman; Booth was shot, and Harold captured, '65.

27. — Blockade of Virginia and North Carolina ports, '61. Union flag raised at New Orleans, '62. Stoneman's raid in Virginia (ended May 8); Gen. Hooker moved on Fredericksburg; Streight's expedition from Tuscumbia, Ala., to Rome, Ga. (captured by Conf. Forrest, May 3), '63.

28. — Forts Jackson and St. Philip surrendered, '62. Hooker crossed the Rappahannock, '63. War department issued orders to reduce army expenses, '65.

29. — Indiana legislature voted $500,000 to arm the state with; first confederate congress at Montgomery, Ala.; Maryland house by 53 to 13, and the senate unanimously, voted against secession, '61. Battle of Fairmont, W. Va.; Porter's fleet bombarded Grand Gulf, Miss., '63. Proclamation by the president removing restrictions on international trade, '65.

30. — Siege of Corinth, Miss., '62. Grant's army landed near Port Gibson, Miss., '63. Action at Jenkin's Ferry, Ark., '64. Paroling of Johnston's troops at Greensboro', '65.

MAY.

1. — Butler occupied New Orleans, '62. Union victory at Port Gibson; beginning of Grant's campaign against Vicksburg, '63. Commodore W. D. Porter died, '64.

2. — The guerrilla Morgan captured Union troops at Pulaski, Tenn., '62. May 2 to 4, battle of Chancellorsville, between Hooker and Lee; confederate victory, '63. Reward of $100,000 offered for capture of Jefferson Davis, '65.

3. — Connecticut voted $2,000,000; Virginia militia called out; President Lincoln called for 42,000 three years' volunteers, '61. Battle of Farmington, Miss., '62. Grant's army crossed the Rapidan toward Chancellorsville and the Wilderness, '64.

4. — Battle of Williamsburg, Va., '62. Siege of Suffolk, Va., raised; end of the battle of Chancellorsville, '63. Reconstruction bill passed, '64. Lincoln buried; Gen. Dick Taylor surrendered, '65.

5. — Battle of Williamsburg, Va., '62. C. L. Vallandigham arrested, '63. Lee attacked Grant at the Wilderness, May 5 to 9; battle of Rocky Face ridge, Ga.; action at Dunn's Bayou, La., '64.

6. — Arkansas seceded, 69 to 1; confederate congress published the war and privateering act, '61. Hooker retreated across the Rappahannock, '63; battle of the Wilderness continued, '64.

7. — Military league formed between Tennessee and the confederacy, '61. Battle of West Point, Va., '62. Kilpatrick's cavalry completed the circuit of Lee's army, '63. Lee

attacked Grant; Butler defeated at Bermuda Hundred; battle of Stony Creek station, Va., '64.

8. — Tennessee seceded, '61. Monitor and gunboats attacked Sewall's Point; battle of McDowell, Va., '62. Bombardment of Port Hudson, '63. Action at Todd's Tavern, Va.; Grant pursued Lee to May 18 to Spottsylvania Court-House, '64.

9. — Confederate congress authorized the president to accept all volunteers, '61. Gen. Hunter issued emancipation proclamation; Pensacola evacuated by the confederates, '62. Virginia battles continued — Swift Creek and Cloyd's mountain; Gen. Sedgwick killed; Sheridan's cavalry raid (9th-13th), '64.

10. — Gen. R. E. Lee put at the head of the confederate army in Virginia, '61. Surrender of Norfolk; Gosport navy yard burned; gunboat battle at Fort Pillow, '62. Stonewall Jackson died; Port Hudson batteries silenced, '63. Battle of Spottsylvania, '64.

11. — Confederates destroyed the Merrimac, '62. Battle of Horse-shoe Bend, Ky., '63. Grant "proposes to fight it out on this line, if it takes all summer;" Butler intrenched at Bermuda Hundred, '64. Davis and Reagan captured at Irwinville, Ga., by Lt.-Col. Pritchard; Jeff Thompson surrendered, '65.

12. — Natchez taken by Union troops, '62. Battle of Raymond, Miss., McPherson defeated the confederates under Gregg, '63. Action at Fort Darling, Va. (12th-16th); Sherman carried the confederate position at Dalton; Conf. Gen. J. E. B. Stuart killed in Va., '64. Engagement near Boco Chico, the last engagement of the war, '65.

13. — Queen Victoria's proclamation of neutrality, '61. Yazoo City, Miss., captured by gunboats, '63. Gen. McPherson captured nine trains of military stores, '64. Action at Palmetto Ranche, Tex., '65. Jefferson Davis released on bail, '67.

14. — Jackson, Miss., captured, '63. Battle of Drury's Bluff, '64

15. — Gov. Hicks of Maryland called for volunteers, '61. Grant defeated Pemberton at Edwards Station, Miss., '63. Union victory at Resaca; Gen. Sigel defeated at Newmarket, Va., '64.

16. — Lincoln nominated for president, '60. Bridges on the Baltimore and Ohio railroad destroyed, '61. Battle at Princeton, W. Va., '62. United States transport Oriental wrecked; Grant defeated Pemberton at Champion Hills, Miss., '63. Fighting (16th-30th) at Bermuda Hundred, Va., '64.

17. — Spies arrested in Washington; confederate congress authorized treasury notes, '61. Confederates driven across the Chickahominy, '62. Battle of Big Black River, Miss., '63. South Carolina union convention at Beaufort; Rome, Ga., captured, '64.

18. — Arkansas admitted to the confederacy; express packages not sent south of Washington, '61. Grant besieged Vicksburg, '63. Action at Calhoun Station, La., '64.

19. — Lincoln revoked Hunter's emancipation proclamation; battle of Searcy Landing, Ark., '62. Blackiston's Island lighthouse destroyed by confederates, '64. Davis arrived at Fortress Monroe, '65.

MAY.

20. — North Carolina seceded; Gov. Magoffin proclaimed Kentucky neutral, '61. Fighting before Vicksburg, '63. Confederates attacked Ames's division of Butler's army, '64. Confederate ram Stonewall surrendered to Spanish authorities in Cuba, '65.

21. — Confederate Congress adjourned, '61.

22. — Union troops destroyed Ship Island fortifications, '61. Grant's attack on Vicksburg repulsed; battle at Gum Swamp, N.C., '63. Southern ports opened, '65.

23. — Part of McClellan's army crossed the Chickahominy; battles at Front Royal, Lewisburg, and Mechanicsville, Va., '62. Action (23d-27th) at North Anna River, Va., '64.

24. — Col. Ellsworth shot at Alexandria; southern mails stopped, '61. Banks retreated to Winchester; battle of the Chickahominy, '62. Sheridan destroyed the Danville railroad near Richmond, '64.

25. — Banks retreated to the Potomac; battle of Winchester, Va., '62. Union victory near Dallas, Ga., '64.

26. — New Orleans blockaded; strong Union vote in West Virginia, '61. Torpedo explosion at Bachelor's Creek, N.C.; fighting (20th-29th) at Decatur and Moulton, Ala.; Louisiana state convention abolished slavery, '64. Gen. E. Kirby Smith and army surrendered to Gen. Canby, '65.

27. — Gen. McDowell put in command at Washington; Mobile blockaded; Mississippi River blockaded, '61. Battle of Hanover Court-House, Va., '62. Bank's assault on Port Hudson repulsed with heavy loss, '63. Lee retreated toward Richmond, '64.

28. — Savannah blockaded, '61. Confederates retreated from Corinth, Miss., '62. First colored regiment from the North left Boston, '63. Action at Salem church, Va.; Sherman repulsed Longstreet's attack at Dallas, '64.

29. — Jefferson Davis reached Richmond, '61. Action near Thoroughfare Gap, Tenn., '63. Grant crossed the Pamunky, '64. President Johnson issued an amnesty proclamation, '65.

30. — Union troops occupied Front Royal; battle at Booneville, Miss., '62. Grant begun earthworks at Vicksburg, '63. Grant repulsed Lee's attack north of the Chickahominy, '64.

31. — Maj.-Gens. Banks and Fremont commissioned, '61. Battle of Seven Pines and Fair Oaks, Va., '62. Fremont nominated for president and Gen. Cochrane for vice-president, '64. Brazil withdrew belligerent rights from the confederates, '65.

JUNE.

1. — Cavalry action at Fairfax Court-House, '61. Battle at Seven Pines, '62. Confederate attack at Cold Harbor defeated, '64. Day of humiliation and prayer on account of Lincoln's death, '65.

2. — Burnside prohibited the circulation of the New York World and Chicago Times in the department of the Ohio, '63. Action at Bermuda Hundred, Va., '64. Kirby Smith and Magruder formally surrendered at Galveston, '65.

3. — Action at Phillippi, W. Va.; Border State Convention, '61. Union troops land on James Island, near Charleston; Lee took command of confederate army, '62. New York supreme court decided against legal-tender notes; convention of New York peace democrats, '63. Battles of Cold Harbor and Panther Gap, '64.

4. — Confederates abandoned and burned Fort Pillow, '62. Burnside's order regarding World and Times revoked; Gillmore relieved Hunter of the department of the South; battle of Franklin, Tenn., '63. Hampton's cavalry defeated at Howe's store, '64.

5. — Raid to Warwick River, Va., '63. Sherman's army fell back toward Atlanta; battle of Piedmont, Va., '64.

6. — Union troops occupied Memphis; fierce gun-boat fight; battle of Harrisonburg, Va., '62. Fight at Milliken's Bend, '63. Action at Lake Chicot, Ark.; night attack on Burnside repulsed, '64.

7. — Confederate battery silenced at Chattanooga; confederate executed for tearing down a Union flag at New

Orleans; battle of Cross Keys, Va., '62. Lincoln and Johnson nominated for president and vice-president; Philadelphia sanitary fair opened; Morgan's raid on Kentucky begun, '64.

8. — Two confederate spies shot at Franklin, Tenn., '63. Sherman's advance on Kenesaw range; Gillmore's raid on Richmond fortifications, '64.

9. — Battle of Fort Republic, Va., '62. Part of Hooker's army crossed the Rappahannock; battle of Beverly Ford, '63; Gen. Burbridge defeated the confederates at Mount Sterling. June 9 to 30, battle of Kenesaw Mountain, '64.

10. — Confederate victory at Big Bethel, '61. Battle of James Island, S.C., '62. Confederate congress adjourned; battle of Brice's Cross Roads, Miss., '64.

11. — Wheeling convention, '61. Democratic peace meeting in Brooklyn, '63. Sheridan's victory at Trevillian Station; action at Cynthiana, Ky., '64.

12. — Confederate privateer Clarence captured six vessels off Chesapeake, '63. Grant crossed the Chickahominy, '64.

13. — Confederate fast day, '61. Battle of Winchester, Va., '63. Fugitive slave law repealed in the house of representatives, 63 to 15; battles of White Oak Swamp Bridge, and Charles City Cross Roads, Va., '64. All ports east of the Mississippi proclaimed to be open, July 1, '65.

14. — Confederates evacuated Harper's Ferry, '61. Banks's attack on Port Hudson repulsed, '63. Grant crossed to the South of the James; Gen. Polk killed, '64.

15. — Lee invaded Maryland; Lincoln called for 100,000 men, '63. Battle of Baylor's Farm; action at Samaria church, Va., '64.

16. — Battle at Secessionville, S.C., '62. Confederate attack on Harper's Ferry defeated, '63. Attack on the Union line at Petersburg repulsed, '64.

17. — West Virginia voted itself independent of the other part of the state; Union victory at Booneville, Mo., '61. Battle at St. Charles, Ark., '62. Confederate ram Atlanta captured by the Weehawken; battle at Aldie, Va., '63. Confederates abandoned intrenchments at Bermuda Hundred; action at Lynchburg, Va., '64. A. H. Stephens and R. E. Lee applied for pardon, '65.

18. — Skirmish before Richmond; Union defeat near Hernando, Miss., '62. Grant's attack on confederate works repulsed, '64.

19. — Confederate cavalry raid into Harrison County, Ind., '63. The Alabama sunk off Cherbourg by the Kearsarge, '64.

20. — McClellan took command in West Virginia, '61. Union troops occupied Holly Springs, Miss., '62. West Virginia admitted to Union; Vicksburg bombarded, '63. Fitzhugh Lee and Hampton repulsed at White House, '64.

21. — East Tennessee Union convention, '61. Battle of Battle Creek, Tenn., '62. Battle of La Fourche Crossing, La.; battle of Upperville, Va., '63. Battle of Davis's Farm, confederate victory, '64.

22. — Skirmish at Frederick, Md., '63. House of representatives resolved to abolish slavery; battle on the Weldon road, '64.

23. — Battle of Big Black River, Mo.; battle of Brashear City, La.; confederates occupied Chambersburg; beginning of Rosecrans's Murfreesboro' campaign, '63. Attack on the Weldon railroad, confederate victory, '64. Presidential proclamation rescinding the blockade on all United States ports, '65.

24. — Tennessee voted itself out of the Union, 104,019 to 47,238, '61. Maryland constitutional convention abolished slavery; confederate victory at Staunton Bridge, '64.

25. — Virginia seceded by vote of 128,884 to 32,134; Iowa issued war loan of $600,000, '61. Beginning of the seven days' battle before Richmond; battle of Mechanicsville; confederates destroyed their gunboats on the Mississippi; Gen. Pope in command of the army of Virginia, '62.

26. — Confederates occupied Gettysburg; death of Admiral Foote, '63.

27. — Bombardment of Vicksburg; Fremont relieved, '62. Battles of Gaines's Mill and Golding's Farm, '63. McPherson's and Thomas's attack southwest of Kenesaw Mountain repulsed, '64.

28. — Battle of Chickahominy, '62. Battle of Donaldsonville, La., '63. Meade superseded Hooker, '63. Battle of Stony Creek, '64.

29. — Battle of Savage's Station, '62. Battle of Reams's Station and of Peach Orchard, '64. Close of the conspirators' trial at Washington, '65.

30. — Battle of White Oak Swamp, '62. Johnston evacuated Kenesaw Mountain; Salmon P. Chase resigned as secretary of the treasury, '64.

JULY.

1. — Lincoln called for 300,000 troops; battle of Malvern Hill; Sheridan defeated Chalmers at Booneville, Miss., '62. Battle of Gettysburg begun; Gen. Reynolds killed, '63. W. P. Fessenden accepted the secretaryship of the treasury, '64.

2. — West Virginia legislature organized at Wheeling; action at Falling Waters, Md., '61. Battle of Gettysburg continued, '63. Confederate Gen. Ewell invaded the Shenandoah Valley in three columns, '64.

3. — Arkansas called out 10,000 men, '61. Battle at Elvington Heights, Va., '62. Union victory at Gettysburg, '63. Travel on B. & O. road stopped; fighting (3d-5th) at Smyrna, Ga., '64.

4. — Executive session of congress; New Hampshire voted $1,000,000 loan, '61. Battle of Helena, Ark.; Vicksburg surrendered to Grant, '63. Mosby's cavalry crossed the Potomac at Point of Rocks, '64.

5. — Battle at Carthage, Missouri, '61. Confederate attack on colored brigade near Port Hudson defeated, '64. July 5 and 6, battle of Jackson, Miss., '64.

6. — Battle of Grand Prairie, Ark., '62. John Morgan's confederates invaded Indiana, '63. Hagerstown, Md., evacuated by Union troops; action (6th-10th) on the Chattahoochee River, Ga., '64.

7. — Union victory at Bayou Cache, Ark., '62. Bragg retreated across the Tennessee River, '63. Confederate raiders held Harper's Ferry, '64. Execution of Harold, Payne, Atzerodt, and Mrs. Surratt, '65.

JULY.

8. — Surrender of Port Hudson; the Mississippi River opened, '63. Gen. Wallace evacuated, and the confederates occupied, Frederick, '64.

9. — Fremont put in command of the Western department, '61. Beginning of actions about Jackson, Miss. (9th-16th), '63. Confederate victory at Monocacy, Md., '64.

10. — Gilmore landed on Morris Island and captured the forts; assault on Fort Wagner, '63. Johnston retreated to the fortifications around Atlanta, '64.

11. — Union victory at Rich Mountain, Va., '61. Halleck appointed commander-in-chief, '62. Destruction of confederate salt-works at Tampa Bay and stores at Dutch Gap, '64.

12. — Morgan invaded Ohio; martial law at Cincinnati, Newport, and Covington, '63. Confederate raid seven miles from Washington, '64.

13. — Battle of Carrickford, W. Va., '61. Confederates captured Murfreesboro', '62. Action at Jackson, Tenn.; draft riot in New York, '63. July 13, 14, and 15, Forrest defeated in five battles, '64.

14. — Battle of Fayetteville, Ark.; Gen. Pope took command of the army of Virginia, '62. Battle of Falling Waters, Md.; battle of Elk River, Tenn.; New York draft riot continued, '63.

15. — Confederate gunboat Arkansas ran the Union fleet and reached Vicksburg, '62. Battle of Halltown, Va.; draft riots in New York, Troy, and Boston, '63.

16. — End of New York draft riot; many rioters killed, '63. Sherman's army crossed the Chattahoochee in pursuit of Johnston, '64.

17. — Battle of Honey Springs, Ind. Ter.; battle of Canton, Miss.; orders issued to enforce the draft at all hazards, '63. Union victory at Grand Gulf, '64.

18. — Confederate victory at Blackburn's Ford, Va., '61. Action at Memphis, Mo., '62. Gillmore's assault on Fort Wagner defeated, '63. Crook defeated Early at Snicker's Gap; Union victory at Peach Tree Creek; call for 500,000 men, '64.

19. — Banks superseded Patterson in command on the Potomac, '61. Battle at Memphis, Tenn., '62. Battle of Buffington Island, O., '63.

20. — Confederate congress met in Richmond, '61. Battle before Atlanta, '64.

21. — Battle of Bull Run — confederate victory, '61.

22. — McClellan put in command of the army of the Potomac, '61. Hood's assault on Sherman at Atlanta defeated; Louisiana state convention adopted constitution abolishing slavery; Gen. McPherson shot in Hood's first sortie from Atlanta, '64.

23. — Battle of Manassas Gap, '63. Gen. Averill defeated at Winchester, Va., '64.

24. — Skirmish with Morgan at Washington, O., '63.

25. — Lincoln's proclamation of the confiscation act, '62.

JULY.

26. — Halleck superseded McClellan, '62. Morgan and all his men captured near New Lisbon, O., '63. Gen. McCook defeated by confederates on the Macon and Western railroad, '64.

27. — Confederate victory at Richmond, Ky., '63. July 27 and 28, battles at Deep Bottom, New Market, and Malvern Hill, Va., '64.

28. — Union victory at Moore's Mills, Mo., '62. Second sortie from Atlanta, '64.

29. — Guerrillas defeated at Mount Sterling, Ky., '62.

30. — Action at Paris, Ky., '62. Lincoln issued an order for retaliation of barbarous treatment, '63. Mine explosion before Petersburg, Va.; Union defeat; Chambersburg burned, '64.

31. — Lee and Meade again on the Rappahannock, '63.

AUGUST.

1. — McClellan reorganized the army, '61. Action at Newark, Mo., '62. Union cavalry victory at Kelly's Ford, '63. Bradley, Johnson, and McCausland defeated at Cumberland, losing part of their plunder from Virginia, '64.

2. — Skirmish at Ozark, Mo., '62. Col. Stout captured by McCausland and Johnson, '64.

3. — Gen. Foster's reconnaissance on the James River, '63.

4. — Confederate ram Arkansas destroyed; Secretary Stanton ordered draft of 300,000 men, '62. McCausland and Johnson defeated at New Creek; Jefferson Davis's sugar-mill at Manitee totally destroyed, '64.

5. — Union victory at Athens, Mo., '61. Gen. McCook murdered while wounded; battle of Baton Rouge; battle of Malvern Hill, '62. Aug. 5 to 23, Farragut's great victory in Mobile Bay, '64.

6. — Hooker abandoned Malvern Hill; battles of Tazewell, Tenn., and Kirksville, Mo., '62. Sherman's unsuccessful assault on Atlanta, '64.

7. — Confederates destroyed Hampton, Va., '61. Confederates advanced across the Rapidan; battle of Trenton, Tenn., '62. Sheridan took command of the middle military division; battle of Moorefield, Va.; McCausland and Johnson defeated by Averill, '64.

8. — Habeas corpus suspended; orders issued to arrest those who discourage enlistments; no passports to be issued, '62. Fort Gaines, in Mobile Bay, surrendered; confed-

AUGUST.

erates withdrew from the Maryland side of the Potomac, '64.

9. — Battle of Cedar Mountain, Va., '62. Butler began Dutch Gap Canal, '64.

10. — Battle of Wilson's Creek, Mo.; Gen. Lyon killed, '61. Battle of Nueces River, Tex., '62. Sherman bombarded Atlanta, '64.

11. — Battle of Independence, Mo., '62. Battle of Sulphur Springs Bridge, Va., '64.

12. — Battle of Gallatin, Tenn., Aug. 12 and 13, '62. Toombs exposed the bankruptcy of the confederacy, '63. Northern New York threatened by an invasion from Canada, '64.

13. — Steamboat collision on the Potomac; 80 soldiers killed, '62. Confederate cavalry captured five Union steamers with cattle at Shawneetown, '64.

14. — Fremont declared martial law in Missouri, '61. Union victory at Strawberry Plains, battle from Aug. 14 to 18, '64.

15. — Jefferson Davis ordered Northern men to leave the South within forty days, '61. Gen. Steadman drove the confederates from Dalton, '64.

16. — Lincoln proclaimed non-intercourse with the confederacy; passport system established, '61. Battle of Lone Jack, Mo.; Cols. Corcoran and Wilcox reached Fortress Monroe from Richmond prison, '62. Battle of Deep Run, '64.

17. — Pope's retreat begun, '62. Union bombardment of Sumter begun, '63.

18. — Union raid in North Carolina, '63. Battle of Six Mile Station on Weldon railroad, N.C., '64.

19. — Union raid on Grenada, Miss., '63. Confederate victory at Six Mile Station; Mosby massacred the wounded and prisoners at Snicker's Gap, Va., '64.

20. — Quantrell, the guerrilla, sacked and burned Lawrence, Kan., and murdered citizens, '63.

21. — Confederate attempt to cross the Rappahannock, '62. Rosecrans attacked Chattanooga, '63. Confederate attack on the Weldon railroad repulsed; battle of Summit Point, Va.; Forrest took Memphis and was driven out, '64. Trial of Wirz, the Andersonville jailer, '65.

22. — Reception to Col. Corcoran in New York, '62. Gen. Jeff C. Thompson and staff captured, '63. Union victory at Canton, Ky.; Johnson, the confederate commander, killed, '64.

23. — Battle of Big Hill, Ky. Fight between Pope and the confederates, '62. Charleston shelled at nearly six miles distance, '63. Fort Morgan surrendered, '64.

24. — Cavalry skirmishes near Fredericksburg and Fairfax, '63. Gens. Heron and Lee took Clinton, Miss.; actions at Bermuda Hundred, Va. (24 and 25), and (24-27) at Halltown, Va., '64.

25. — Confederate attack on Donelson, '62. Battle of Reams's Station — Hancock lost heavily; battle of Smithfield, Va., '64.

26. — Union expedition sailed for Fort Hatteras, N.C., '61. Confederates took Manassas Junction, '62. Battle of

Rocky Gap, Va., '63. Kilpatrick's raid on the Macon railroad, '64.

27. — Battle of Bull Run Bridge, Va.; battle of Kettle Run, Va., '62. John B. Floyd died, '63.

28. — Bombardment and capture of Forts Hatteras and Clark, '61. Second battle of Manassas, '62. Early driven through Smithfield, '64.

29. — Battle at Groveton and Gainsville, Va.; battle at Manchester, Tenn., '62. McClellan nominated for president and Pendleton for vice-president, '64.

30. — Second battle of Bull Run, confederate victory; battles of Bolivar, Tenn., and of Richmond, Ky., '62. Sherman put his whole army between Atlanta and Hood at Jonesboro', '64.

31. — Fort Smith, Ark., captured by Gen. Blunt, '63. Battle of Jonesboro', Ga., Aug. 31 and Sept. 1, '64.

SEPTEMBER.

1. — Battle of Chantilly, Va.; Gens. Kearney and Stevens killed; Burnside evacuated Fredericksburg; battle of Britton's Lane, Tenn., '62. Hood evacuated Atlanta, '64. Removal of all restrictions on Southern ports, '65.

2. — McClellan assigned to command the defences of Washington, '62. Confederates before Petersburg cheered McClellan's nomination; Atlanta captured by Sherman, '64.

3. — Union cavalry victory near Murfreesboro'; Union victories at Darkesville and Perryville, Va., '64.

4. — Oreto ran the blockade into Mobile, '62. Burnside occupied Knoxville, '63. Morgan was routed and killed by Gen. Gillam at Greenville, Tenn., '64.

5. — Confederates invaded Maryland, '62. Women's bread riot in Mobile, '63.

6. — First capture by the Alabama (the whaler Oemulgee); battle of Washington, N.C., '62. Morris Island evacuated by the confederates, '63. Battle of Matamoros, '64.

7. — Gen. Pope relieved of command of the army of Virginia, '62. Union troops captured Fort Wagner, S.C., '63. Confederate Gen. Dibbles surprised at Readyville, '64.

8. — Gen. Lee's proclamation to Maryland, '62. Confederate Col. Jessie and 100 men captured near Ghent, Ky., '64.

9. — Confederates evacuated Fredericksburg, '62. Cumberland Gap captured by Gen. Shackleford, '63. Sherman concentrated near Atlanta, '64.

10. — Rosecrans defeated Floyd at Carnifex Ferry, Va., '61. Levy *en masse* in Pennsylvania to repel invasion, '62. Grant advanced his permanent line half a mile, '64.

11. — Hagerstown, Md., occupied by confederates, '62. Little Rock, Ark., occupied by Union troops, '63.

12. — Hooker occupied Frederick City, Md., '62. Failure of the Sabine Pass expedition, '63.

13. — Fight at Middleton, Md., '62. Harper's Ferry battle, Sept. 12 to 15, '62.

14. — Battle of South Mountain, Va.; battle of Mumfordsville, Ky., Sept. 14 to 16, '62. Price and 10,000 men crossed the White River for Missouri, '64. Chiefs of the rebel Indians renounced the confederacy, '65.

15. — Harper's Ferry surrendered to the confederates; attempt to blockade the Ohio River, '62. Lincoln suspended the habeas corpus act, '63.

16. — Skirmishes at Chattanooga, '63. Thirteenth Pennsylvania regiment and 2,500 cattle captured at Sycamore church; action (16th-18th) at Fort Gibson, I.T., '64.

17. — Battle of Antietam; Union troops evacuated Cumberland Gap, '62.

18. — Maryland legislature closed by the provost-marshal, and all the confederate sympathizers sent to Fort McHenry, '61. Confederates evacuated Sharpsburg and recrossed the Potomac, '62. Gen. Averill drove the confederates out of Martinsburg, '64.

19. — Battle of Iuka, Miss.; confederates evacuated Harper's Ferry, '62. Beginning of the battle of Chickamau-

ga, '63. Battle of Winchester; Sheridan sent Early "whirling up the valley:" battle at Powder Mill, or Little Rock River, '64.

20. — Confederate Gen. Price captured Col. Mulligan at Lexington, Mo., '61. Battle of Blackburn's Ford, Va., '62. Confederate victory at Chickamauga, '63. Forrest captured Athens, Ala., '64.

21. — John C. Breckenridge joined the confederacy; engagement at Osceola, Mo., '61. Rosecrans retreated from Chickamauga to Chattanooga, '63.

22. — Lincoln's emancipation proclamation issued, '62. Sheridan's victory at Fisher's Hill, '64.

23. — Meade's army reached the Rapidan, '63. Price occupied Bloomfield, Mo., '64.

24. — Count de Paris and the Duc de Chartres became aides to McClellan; great review at Washington, '61. Convention of loyal governors at Altoona, Pa., '62.

25. — Mosby broke the railroad near Fairfax, '63.

26. — Federal fast day, '61. Early retreated to Brown's Gap in the Blue Ridge; battle of Pilot Knob, Mo., '64.

27. — Fremont opened his campaign, '61. Augusta, Ky., destroyed by the confederates, '62. Three Union companies of 39th Missouri regiment at Centralia massacred by Price, '64.

28. — Confederate attack on Burnside near Knoxville repulsed, '63. Battle of New Market Heights; night attack on Hancock's front on Jerusalem plankroad repulsed, '64.

29. — Gen. Davis shot Gen. Nelson at Cincinnati; Union defeat above Port Hudson, '63.

30. — Battle of Newtonia, Mo., '62. Confederate cavalry defeated at Harrison's Landing, Tenn., '63. Renewed fighting at New Market Heights, confederate victory; action at Poplar Springs church, Va., '64.

OCTOBER.

1. — Lincoln visited McClellan's army and urged movement across the Potomac; battle of Shepardstown, Va.; Buell's army left Louisville, '62. Battle of Anderson's Gap, Tenn., '63.

2. — Union victory at Anderson's Cross Roads, Ky., '63. Battle of Saltville, Va., '64.

3. — Union victory at Greenbrier, Va., '61. Battle of Corinth; Gen. Morgan retreated from Cumberland Gap, '62. Sherman crossed the Chattahoochee with 15 days' rations, '64.

4. — Battle of Buffalo Hill, Ky., '61. Confederates defeated at Corinth, '62. Pour steamers burned at St. Louis by fire-bugs, '63.

5. — Gen. Robert Anderson in command in Kentucky, '61. Battle of Metamora, Miss., Union troops occupied Galveston, '62. Confederates bombarded Chattanooga from Lookout Mountain, '63. Hood captured the garrisons of Big Shanty and Ackworth; battle of Allatoona, Ga.; Sheridan's victory at Tom's Brook, '64.

6. — McClellan ordered to cross the Potomac and to give battle, '62. Action at Baxter Springs, Ark., '63. Hood's attack on Allatoona repulsed, '64.

7. — Battle of La Vergne, Tenn., '62. Confederate steamers destroyed on the Red River, '63. Battle of Darleytown Road and New Market Heights; pirate Florida captured at Bahia Bay, by U.S. steamer Wachusett, and sunk, '64.

OCTOBER.

8. — Battle of Perryville, Ky., '62. Union victories near Farmingham, Ky., and Salem, Miss., '63. Union victory at Woodville, '64.

9. — Union forces advanced beyond the Potomac; action at Santa Rosa, Fla., '61. Battle of Lawrenceburg, Ky., '62. Defeat of confederate operations against Rosecrans, '63. Battle of Boonesville, Mo., 9th to 11th; action at Strasburg, Va., '64.

10. — Battle of Harrodsburg, Ky.; Stuart's cavalry raid in Maryland and Pennsylvania, '62. Battle of Blue Springs, Tenn., '63.

11. — Steamer Nashville escaped from Charleston, '61. Confederate Gen. Buford and 1,200 cavalry crossed the Cumberland River at Harpeth Shoals, '64.

12. — Stuart's cavalry recrossed the Potomac, '62. Battle of Ingham's Mills, Miss.; Mead withdrew to the north bank of the Rappahannock; battle of Merrill's Crossing, Mo., '63. Drawn battle of three hours at Strasburg, between Longstreet and Sheridan, '64. Proclamation ending martial law in Kentucky, '65.

13. — Gen. Bragg evacuated Camp Dick Robinson, '62. Battle of Catlett's Station, '63.

14. — Fight at Bristow Station, '63.

15. — Three steamers from New York pursued the Nashville; battle of Lime Creek, Mo., '61. Draft in Boston and Baltimore, '62. Battle at McLean's Ford, Va., '63. Action at Glasgow, Mo., '64.

16. — Confederate raid on Brownsville, Miss., '63.

17. — Battle of Ironton, Mo., 17th to 21st, '61. Lincoln called for 300,000 men, '63. Price occupied Lexington, Mo., '64.

18. — Morgan occupied Lexington, Ky., '62. Maj.-Gen. Birney died at Philadelphia, '64.

19. — Fight near Nashville, '62. Lee recrossed the Rappahannock and marched south, '63. Battle of Cedar Creek; Sheridan's arrival from Winchester (11½ miles away) turned defeat to victory, '64.

20. — Grant succeeded Rosecrans; Battle of Philadelphia, Tenn., '63. Early retreated by night to Mount Jackson, '64.

21. — Battle of Ball's Bluff; Gen. Baker killed; Gen. Zollicoffer defeated at Wild Cat, Ky.; Union victory at Fredericktown, '61. Confederates left West Virginia, '62. Battle of Cherokee Station, Ala., '63. Battle of the Little Blue, Mo., '64.

22. — Confederate salt-works in Florida destroyed, '62. Skirmishes at Columbia and Kingston Spring, Tenn., '63.

23. — Union victory at Maysville, Ark.; battle of Pocotaligo, S.C., '62. Fight at Beverley Ford on the Rappahannock, '63. Battle of Independence, Mo., '64.

24. — Rosecrans succeeded Buell over the army of Kentucky, '62.

25. — Major Zagonyi's charge at Springfield, Mo., '61. Fight near Manassas, '62. Battle of Pine Bluff, Ark., '63. Price defeated with loss of camp equipage at Fort Scott road, '64.

OCTOBER.

26. — Battle of Romney, W. Va., '61. McClellan's advance begun, '62. Grant moved on Lookout Mountain, '63. Pleasonton defeated Price at Mine Creek; Marmaduke and Cabell captured, '64.

27. — Battle of Labadiesville, La., '62. Battle of Wauhatchie, Tenn., '63. Hooker defeated the confederates at Brown's Ferry, '63. Grant's attack on the South side railroad failed; battle of Hatcher's Run, Va.; battle of Fair Oaks, Va., Oct. 27 and 28, '64.

28. — Capture of Lookout Mountain by Grant; afterward abandoned and occupied by the confederates, '63. Confederate ram Albemarle destroyed by a torpedo boat on the Roanoke River, '64.

29. — Great naval expedition under Dupont from Fortress Monroe, '61. Rhoddy's attack on Col. Morgan's colored troops at Decatur, Ala., repulsed, '64.

30. — Gen. Mitchell died at Port Royal, '62. Heavy bombardment of Charleston, '63.

31. — Skirmish at Maysville, Ky. Bank's expedition landed at Brazos Island, '62.

NOVEMBER.

1. — Gen. Winfield Scott resigned as commander-in-chief, and General McClellan succeeded him, '61.

2. — Gen. Fremont removed; steamer Bermuda ran the Savannah blockade, '61. Gen. Foster's expedition left Newbern, '62. Union victory at Roan Springs, Tenn.; boat attack on Sumter failed, '63. National thanksgiving for peace, '65.

3. — Union rising in East Tennessee, '61. Battle at Grand Coteau, La.; actions at Columbia and Colliersville, Tenn., '63. Ram Albemarle destroyed, '64.

4. — Grant's army occupied Lagrange, Miss.; Georgia salt-works destroyed, '62. Banks's expedition occupied Brownsville, '63.

5. — Order issued for the removal of McClellan; battle of Nashville, Tenn., '62. Confederates shelled Chattanooga, '63. Butler took command of troops in New York City, '64.

6. — Lincoln elected, '61. McClellan's advance occupied Warrenton, Va.; battle of Garrettsburg, Ky., '62. Guerrillas plundered Blandville, Ky.; battle of Droop Mountain, Va., '63. Confederate ram Shenandoah surrendered in the Mersey to an English man-of-war, '65.

7. — Brig.-Gen. Grant commanded at battle of Belmont, Mo., '61. McClellan removed and Burnside appointed; battle of Marianna, Ark.; negro troops engaged at Port Royal, '62. Meade's army engaged the confederates at Kelly's Ford and Rapidan Station, '63.

NOVEMBER.

8. — Mason and Slidell taken, '61. Battle of Hudsonville, Miss., '62. Lincoln and Johnson elected, '64. McClellan resigned commission; Sheridan made major-general of regular army, '64.

9. — Butler's sequestration order issued, '62. Meade in line of battle, '63. Sherman issued marching order for advance through Georgia, '64.

10. — Senator Chestnut of South Carolina resigned; bill in the South Carolina legislature for 10,000 volunteers, '60. Union demonstration in Memphis, '62. Confederates concentrated on the south bank of the Rapidan, '63. Night fighting before Richmond, '64. Execution of Captain Wirz, '65.

11. — Senator Hammond of South Carolina resigned, '60. Gen. Halleck in command of the Western department, '61. Charleston and Sumter shelled regularly, '63.

12. — Union meeting in Arkansas, '63. About 10,000 prisoners exchanged near Fort Pulaski; Atlanta evacuated by the confederates, '64.

13. — Holly Springs, Miss., occupied by Union troops, '62. Confederates across the Potomac at Edward's Ferry, '63. Gen. Gillam defeated with heavy loss at Bull's Gap, '64.

14. — Gen. Stahel's forces passed Snicker's Gap, '62. Longstreet forced Burnside back at Knoxville; battle of Huff's Ferry, Tenn., '63.

15. — Great public meeting at Mobile declared the causes of secession, '60. Frigate San Jacinto brought Mason and Slidell, taken from the English steamer Trent, to Fortress Monroe, '61. Action at Fayetteville, Va., '62.

16. — Order for Sabbath observance issued, '62. Battle of Campbell's Station, Tenn.; Sherman's corps joined Thomas at Chattanooga, '63. Sherman left Atlanta on his march to the sea, '64.

17. — Artillery fight near Fredericksburg, '62. Siege of Knoxville, Tenn., begun; battle of Mustang Island, Tex., '63. Gen. Slocum burned the railroad station at Locust Circle, '64.

18. — Georgia voted $1,000,000 for arming the State; Maj. Anderson ordered to Fort Moultrie, '60. Burnside advanced opposite Fredericksburg, '62. Slocum cut the Macon railroad; the Georgia legislature fled from Milledgeville, '64.

19. — Executive session of the Louisiana legislature ordered, '60. Confederate congress met, '61. Gettysburg cemetery dedicated, '63. Madison captured and burned by Sherman, '64.

20. — Bank suspensions in Richmond, Baltimore, Washington, Philadelphia, Trenton, and the South, '60. Missouri confederate legislature passed secession ordinance, '61. Gen. Howard captured Milledgeville, '64.

21. — Surrender of Fredericksburg demanded, '62. Union victory at Liberty, '64. Sherman defeated Wheeler's cavalry at Gordon, '64.

22. — Order issued for the release of all State prisoners, '62. Part of Knoxville burned, '63. Action at Griswoldville, Ga., '64.

23. — Action at Fort Pickens, Fla., '61. Reconnaissance in force by Thomas at Chattanooga, '63.

NOVEMBER.

24. — Mason and Slidell put in Fort Warren, '61. Capture of Lookout Mountain; Hooker's fight above the clouds, '63. Potomac, James, and Valley armies celebrated Thanksgiving with delicacies from the North, '64.

25. — Raid on Pooleville, Md.; Confederates attacked Newbern, '62. Capture of Missionary Ridge, '63. Confederate attempt to burn New York, '64.

26. — Lincoln visited Burnside; Sherman left Memphis, '62. Meade crossed the Rapidan, '63. Action at Sylvan Grove (26th-29th), and Browne's Cross Roads, Va. Beauregard's siege of Decatur repulsed, Nov. 26 to 29, '64.

27. — Fighting between Meade and Lee, near Mine Run, Va.; battle of Ringgold and Taylor's Ridge, Ga.; steamer Greyhound burned on the James River, '64.

28. — Burnside visited Washington; battle of Cone Hill, Ark.; confederate cavalry crossed the Rappahannock, '62. Morgan and six officers escaped from the Ohio penitentiary, '63.

29. — Mississippi sent commissioners to the other Southern States, '60. Union victory at Frankfort, W. Va., '62. Longstreet's attack on Knoxville repulsed, '63. Action (29th, 30th) at Spring Hill, Tenn., '64.

30. — Jefferson Davis elected president of the confederacy for six years, '61. Battle of Franklin; Hood repulsed with heavy loss; Attorney-General Bates resigned; Roger A. Pryor captured; battle of Grahamsville, S.C.; battle of Honey Hill, S.C., '64.

DECEMBER.

1. — Great secession meeting at Memphis, '60. Meade recrossed the Rapidan, '63. Banks resumed command of the department of the Gulf, '64.

2. — Confederates in Tennessee and Mississippi retreated before Grant, Dec. 1 to 3, '62. Confederate Gen. Hardee superseded Bragg in Georgia; battle of Walker's Ford, W. Va., '63.

3. — Gen. Geary occupied Winchester, Va., '62. Union foray toward Canton, Miss., '63.

4. — John C. Breckenridge unanimously expelled from the U. S. senate, '61. Longstreet abandoned the siege of Knoxville, '63.

5. — Confederate victory at Coffeeville, Miss., '62. Confederate attack on Murfreesboro' blockhouses repulsed, '64.

6. — Skirmish near Lebanon, Tenn., '62. Ex-secretary Chase appointed justice of the supreme court; capture of Pocotaligo bridge, S.C.; action (6th-9th) at Deveaux's Neck, S.C., '64.

7. — Gen. Butler's expedition at Port Royal, '61. Union victory at Prairie Grove, Ark., '62. Electoral colleges met; Forrest routed by Rousseau near Murfreesboro', '64.

8. — Lincoln issued amnesty proclamation, '63. Confederates established a battery on the Cumberland River; action at Hatcher's Run, Va., '64.

9. — Congress authorized the exchange of prisoners; Confederate congress admitted Kentucky to the confeder-

acy, '61. Direct communication established with Sherman near Savannah, '64.

10. — Howell Cobb, secretary of the treasury, resigned; Senator Clay of Alabama resigned; Louisiana legislature appropriated $500,000, '60. Battle of Union gunboats and confederate batteries at Port Royal, Va., '62. Gunboat Otsego sunk by confederate torpedo on the Roanoke River, '64.

11. — Bombardment of Fredericksburg, '62. Battles of Bean Station and Morristown, Tenn. (10th-14th), '63.

12. — Burnside occupied Fredericksburg, '62. Col. Morgan was captured at Kingston, Tenn., '64.

13. — First military execution; Deserter Johnson shot; engagement at Buffalo Mountain, W. Va., '61. Confederate victory at Fredericksburg, '62. Gen. Hazen captured Fort McAllister, '64.

14. — Lewis Cass, secretary of state, resigned, '60. Union victory near Kingston, N.C., '62. Union victory at Bean Station, Va., '63. Gen. Dix ordered operations against the confederates on the Canadian frontier, '64.

15. — Retreat of Burnside; the advance of Banks's expedition arrived at New Orleans, '62. Victory of Gen. Thomas near Nashville; raid of Stoneman in southwest Virginia; Forrest defeated near Murfreesboro', '64.

16. — Burnside retreated across the Rappahannock; Banks put in command of the department of the Gulf, '62. Hood routed near Nashville, '64.

17. — Union victory at Mumfordville, Ky., '61. Baton Rouge occupied by Union troops, '62. Resolutions offered

in the confederate house to send peace commissioners to Washington, '64.

18. — Battle of Milford, Mo., '61. Confederates seized Lexington, Ky.; Quantrell defeated by Phillips's Indian brigade near Fort Gibson, '62. Secretary Seward required all persons coming to the United States, except immigrants, to have passports, '64.

19. — End, at Oxford, Miss., of successful six days' raid of Col. Dickey's scouting party, '62. Battle of Barren Fork, Ind. Territory; confederates repulsed Standthwaite's attack on Fort Gibson, Ark., '63. Draft and call for 300,000 men, '64.

20. — South Carolina seceded, '60. Battle at Drainesville, Va., '61. Gen. Foster returned to Newbern after a successful expedition; Holly Springs, Miss., sacked by confederates; Sherman's army embarked at Memphis for Vicksburg, '62. Hardee evacuated Savannah; navy yard burned, and salt-works blown up, '64.

21. — Fight on Wolf River, Miss., '61. Sherman occupied Savannah, '64.

22. — Confederate success in Isle of Wight Court-House (Va.); skirmish, '62. Gen. Corcoran killed by fall from his horse, '63.

23. — Union troops occupied Winchester, Va., '62. Union raid on Luray, '63. Fight near Gordonsville, Va., '64.

24. — Ten miles of railroad destroyed west of Vicksburg, '62. Choctaw Indians deserted the confederacy, '63. Porter's fleet attacked Fort Fisher, '64.

25. — Skirmish at Bacon Creek, Ky., '62. British bark Circassian seized in the North River by a U. S. marshal, '63. Porter's attack on Fort Fisher repulsed, '64.

26. — Maj. Anderson and 80 men went to Fort Sumter, '60. Sherman disembarked at Yazoo, '62. The ironclad Dictator launched at New York, '63.

27. — Mason and Slidell were surrendered to the British minister, '61. Sherman marched on Vicksburg; action at Dumfries, Va., '62.

28. — South Carolina seized the U. S. custom-house, post-office, and arsenal, '60. Action at Mt. Zion, Mo., '61. Battle of Chickasaw Bayou, Vicksburg; Gen. Blunt captured Van Buren, Ark.; battle of Elk Fork, Tenn., '62. Action at Charleston, Tenn., '63. Reconstruction meeting at Savannah, '64.

29. — J. B. Floyd, secretary of war, resigned, '60. Sherman repulsed at Vicksburg with heavy loss, '62.

30. — Sherman raised the siege of Vicksburg; battles of Jefferson and of Parker's Cross Roads, Tenn.; Monitor foundered off Hatteras, '62. Great naval expedition left New Orleans, '63.

31. — Battle of Stone River, or Murfreesboro', begun; McClernand succeeded Sherman before Vicksburg, '62. Large quantity of confederate money seized in New York, '63.